WELCOME TO CASTLE CAMPBELL

Everyone is awe-struck by Castle Campbell. It stands in solemn and lofty isolation upon a narrow ridge, overlooked by the crescent of the Ochil Hills, from which it is separated by a precipitous ravine on each side. At the bottom of these ravines the rushing waters of the Burn of Care and Burn of Sorrow can be glimpsed through deep fissures in the rock. To the south, a gap in the Ochils reveals a splendid view over the town of Dollar.

The stronghold came into the possession of the chief of Clan Campbell in the 1460s. Over the next two centuries the Campbells played leading roles in Scotland's history, and continued to occupy their Lowland seat until it was severely damaged in 1654, during Cromwell's occupation of Scotland.

Above: The octagonal stair tower leading to the great hall in the south range.

CONTENTS

Opposite: The loggia, added around 1590 as a feature of the east range.

CASTLE CAMPBELL AT A GLANCE

Castle Campbell was built to serve three main purposes: to provide accommodation for a leading member of the aristocracy and his extensive household; to provide adequate defence for them; and to look impressive, a conspicuous statement of its lord's wealth and power. The level of importance of these needs fluctuated, though in general, as time went on, comfort and architectural elegance overtook defensibility.

The accommodation required was extensive. There had to be not only a residence for the lord and his immediate family, but also lodgings for his extensive household, from high-ranking officials to menials, as well as guests. These included royalty, who likewise had large travelling households. Castle Campbell shows how these needs were originally met, and also how they changed over time, to meet the increasing aspirations of comfort and privacy.

Opposite: An engraving of the castle by David Octavius Hill, who later became famous as a pioneer of photography.

THE TOWER HOUSE

7   THE HEADLESS GRYPHON
The last surviving remnant of an ornately embellished parapet.

9   THE GREEN MEN
Two carved masonry masks in the top floor ceiling.

8   THE PIT PRISON

A glimpse into the grim conditions endured by prisoners of low status.

THE SOUTH RANGE

11   THE HALL
Once the grandest chamber in the whole castle, commanding superb views over the glen.

11   THE CAMPBELL SHIELDS
A mark of pride and ownership, carved into the stone lintel above the west entrance.

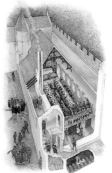

THE EAST RANGE

13 THE LOGGIA

An ornate arcade of a style very rare in Scotland.

13 THE MOULDED STRING COURSE
One of the distinctive features of the range's superior masonry work.

THE GREAT OUTDOORS

31 THE WALK UP DOLLAR GLEN
A circular route from the town takes in the dramatic scenery and ancient woodland of the precipitous glen.

14 THE VIEW FROM THE TOP
If you've come by foot, you'll feel you've earned it. If not, you'll still be impressed.

14 THE GARDENS
The tiered lawns south of the castle provide a hint of the leisured lifestyle once enjoyed by the Campbells.

Entrance

1

2

4

3

5

6

N

A SHORT TOUR OF CASTLE CAMPBELL

This tour guides the visitor around the castle, beginning at the entrance gateway on the north side and ending at 'John Knox's Pulpit' on the south. The tour begins with the four-storey tower in the NE corner of the courtyard, the 1st Earl's private residence. It then moves to the state apartment in the south range, added around 1500 by the 2nd Earl. Finally, it visits the east range, reconstructed by the 7th Earl around 1590. This was as part of a larger scheme to maintain the 150-year-old castle's suitability as an aristocratic residence.

Illustration key

1 Main entrance
2 Tower
3 South range
4 East range
5 Gardens
6 'John Knox's Pulpit'

THE ENTRANCE FRONT

T he grassy knoll on which the tower stands may be the remains of the motte, or mound, on which the first timber castle was built. Across the promontory, there is the hint of a ditch, which would have provided a defensive barrier on this vulnerable landward side.

Below: The main entrance at the north of the castle.

The thick stone wall enclosing the castle courtyard was built in the 15th century. The projecting entrance, though, appears to be later. Two wide-mouthed gunholes – which became fashionable in the 16th century – flank the gateway. The gate doors were strengthened from behind by a timber drawbar, the deep slot for which is visible in the passage. Also in the passage are a stone bench and a locker. The guardroom (now the castle shop) was originally reached from the west (right) side of the passage.

All of this provided an essentially passive form of defence, sufficient to repel a lightly-armed raid, but certainly not enough to withstand a siege supported by artillery. In an age when clan feuds often led to armed hostility, such defences were perfectly adequate.

THE TOWER

T he tower is characteristically 15th-century, with a simple oblong plan and thick walls pierced by few windows. The parapet overhangs the walls and is carried on a single projecting corbel course. At the angles are projecting roundels. Water-spouts carved in the shape of mythical beasts drained the parapet, and one of them, a headless gryphon, survives on the NW roundel. The parapet is not original to the 15th-century tower but a later refinement.

Originally, the tower had two entrances. The one in the west face was primarily a service entrance. The principal entrance was on the south side at first-floor level. When the courtyard was later lowered, the threshold of the service entrance was lowered as well; the present timber stair takes visitors in at the original level.

The doorway opens into a short passage, from which a straight flight of stairs leads to the upper floor. Beyond the passage is a vaulted storage cellar with slit windows in its south wall. After the spiral stair was added, around 1590, one of these windows was enlarged to form a doorway onto the stair.

Above: The west entrance to the tower. Originally this was a service entrance, with the main entrance around the corner.

Below: A cutaway drawing shows the interior of the tower as it might have looked after the present stair was added around 1590.

Above: A headless gryphon is all that survives of the four carved water-spouts.

7

THE UPPER FLOORS

The first-floor room in the tower was the hall. The fireplace occupies much of the east wall. The main window is in the south wall, overlooking the courtyard; like many of the windows in the tower it was later widened. The ogee-arched recess in the north wall was where the lord's best tableware would have been displayed.

The main entrance into the tower opens into this hall at the SE corner, next to the fireplace. This entrance was originally reached from the courtyard by a forestair, but this was replaced by the present stair around 1590. In the corner between the entrance and the fireplace is a poky prison; the hole in the floor gave access to an even pokier 'pit' below.

The lord was responsible for local law enforcement: he had offending freemen put into the prison and serfs into the pit.

The upper floors and parapet were originally reached by a narrow spiral stair in the SW corner of the hall. This went out of use when the new stair was added. The upper levels of the old stairwell were then converted into small closets.

Below: The upper two floors of the tower, before the timber floor was reinstated between them, as drawn by R. W. Billings around 1850.

The room above the hall was the outer of two private family chambers in the tower. This room has a timber ceiling carried on corbels which, for no obvious reason, are more widely spaced in the eastern half of the room.

The fireplace in the north wall has a small salt-box in its right side. In the wall to the right is a latrine closet with a toilet seat, lamp-recess and wash-hand basin. There was originally another wall closet in the SE corner, but this was largely removed when a new doorway was slapped through from the later stair around 1590. This was once a sleeping closet; a more complete bed closet can be seen on the floor above.

This top floor housed the inner family chamber, probably the lord's bedchamber. It was altered around 1590, when the present doorway from the stair was created, entering through what had originally been the earl's bed closet.

The stone vault over the room, also of 1590, has cross-ribs, with a ridge-rib running from end to end. Its highlight is a pair of 'green man' masks: oil-lamps would have been suspended from their mouths. When the vault was inserted, the south window was blocked and a smaller one opened through the north wall. There is a latrine closet in the NE corner.

Top: The prison on the same level as the hall.

Middle: The trapdoor leading to the pit prison below.

Bottom: One of the two 'green man' masks on the ceiling of the top floor.

THE SOUTH RANGE

The range along the south side of the courtyard was built by the 2nd Earl around 1500. It provided an altogether more impressive and commodious environment than the old tower, much better suited for a leading nobleman of the realm. This included an impressive state apartment on the first floor comprising kitchen, hall, outer chamber and inner bedchamber, with a wardrobe and more private family rooms above.

The ground floor, set below the courtyard level, has five stone-vaulted storage cellars, each with a slit window and stone benching along the side walls. The cellars were entered from a covered passage (now open to the elements), while a vaulted pend at the west end gave access to the gardens to the south.

The state apartment on the first floor was reached from the courtyard by two projecting stair towers. The main (public) entrance was by the west stair, which gave access to the 'lower' end of the hall and kitchen on the first floor and the wardrobe and other chambers above the kitchen.

Below: The row of windows along the south wall of the south range would have provided a superb view down the glen.

Carved on the door lintel are three shields. There was also an armorial panel near the top, below the octagonal caphouse. The east stair, later absorbed within the remodelled east range, was for the family's exclusive use. It gave access into both the state apartment and the private family rooms above. The two stair towers were linked horizontally by a gallery directly above the cellar passage.

In its overall design, and in the details of the west stair tower, this range bears a striking resemblance to the King's Old Building, the royal lodging built for James IV at Stirling Castle in the 1490s. The 2nd Earl would have witnessed this being built, and used, and was clearly influenced by it when planning his new lodging. Today the upper floors of this south range are largely ruined, but the first floor layout can still be seen.

The hall at the centre of the first floor was the first in a sequence of three state rooms. It has a fine row of windows overlooking the gardens to the south, the largest of which lit the 'top' end of the hall, where the lord would have sat on his ornate chair of state. A large fireplace in the north wall heated the room, and the recess to its right was the buffet, displaying the best tableware. To its east was the second room in the sequence – 'My Lordis uttir [outer] chalmer'; and the third room – 'My Lordis Inner bed chalmer' – was at the east end. Each room has a large south-facing window, a fireplace and a privy.

Above (left): Inside one of the storage cellars.

Above: An artist's impression of the King's Old Building at Stirling Castle, which almost certainly inspired the architecture of the south range.

Below: Three carved Campbell shields can still be made out on the stair-tower lintel.

DID YOU KNOW...

Visitors frequently ask about the whereabouts of the castle's well. The simple answer is we don't know. Somewhere under the cobbles in the courtyard seems the most likely location. Perhaps when the courtyard is excavated we'll find it.

THE EAST RANGE

I n its present form, the east range dates from around 1590. However, the thick lower walls indicate that it incorporated earlier buildings. This range may well have been the site of the original outer, or great, hall, subsequently replaced by the hall in the state apartment.

The remodelled east range was a sophisticated piece of design. Its courtyard elevation was constructed of fine stone ashlars with narrow joints. Each storey was defined by a moulded string-course, and had nicely proportioned two-light windows. The private stair into the south range was remodelled, and a new stair added to the south face of the old tower. Between the stairs, two corridors gave horizontal access to the old tower, the south range and the east range. These corridors were more than mere passages, however; they were galleries ('the little galrie' on the top floor, 'the laiche galrie' below), where the family could take their exercise in inclement weather, while admiring portraits of the family hanging from the side walls. This was the origin of today's portrait galleries.

At ground level was a loggia, or open arcade, formed of two segmental arches carried on a central pier of clustered shafts. Such arcades were rare in Scotland. Examples also exist at Huntly Castle, seat of the Gordon Earls of Huntly, and St Andrews, residence of the archbishop. The two ground-floor rooms behind the loggia are covered by ribbed vaults similar to that inserted over the top storey in the tower. They probably date from the programme of remodelling around 1590.

Above: The loggia, a very unusual feature in Scotland.

Opposite: Looking down over the east and south ranges from the top of the tower.

Below: An artist's impression of the loggia that was once a feature of St Andrews Castle.

THE GARDENS AND 'JOHN KNOX'S PULPIT'

To the south of the castle are the terraced gardens. These were an important adjunct to the property, for the exclusive use of the Campbells and their guests. Here they would have strolled and sat, taking in the stunning views and conversing privately, whilst smelling the sweet fragrance of the flowers and herbs. The colourful spectacle was also intended to be enjoyed by them from the comfort of their halls and chambers. Though the gardens have never been archaeologically investigated, we can imagine them formally laid out, with raised flower beds and gravelled walks.

Complementing the pleasure garden would have been a kitchen garden, providing vegetables, herbs and fruit for the earl's table. This was probably sited to the west of the castle and reached via the doorways on the west side of the courtyard.

At the SW corner of the garden is a tiny rock pillar, separated from the garden by a deep fissure in the rock called Kemp's Score. The pillar, on which is a stone archway of dubious origin, is affectionately known as 'John Knox's Pulpit'. Local tradition holds that during his stay at the castle the fiery Protestant preached from here to a large congregation.

Kemp's Score itself is said to have been cut by the giant robber, Kemp, who was caught and killed here after stealing the king's dinner from Dunfermline Castle. This and other place-names associated with Castle Campbell, including especially the Burns of Care and Sorrow, are suitably romantic and intriguing, perfectly complementing the dramatically sited ruined castle.

Opposite: The castle seen from the gardens.

THE STORY OF
CASTLE
CAMPBELL

C astle Campbell dates from the 15th century, but the strategic location it commands may have been fortified well before then. The present tower stands on a grassy mound that may have originated as a motte – or castle mound – of a type introduced to Scotland by Anglo-Norman and Flemish settlers in the 12th century. The architecture of the existing tower suggests it was built in the early 15th century. Its simple oblong form, thick walls and few windows were features typical of this earliest generation of Scottish tower houses.

The first mention of the castle is in a papal bull of 1466 which condemned Walter Stewart of Lorn for destroying a 'certain manor with a tower of the Place of Glowm situated in the territory of Dollar'. Stewart was then at feud with the Campbells over the disputed estates of his kinsman John Stewart, Lord of Lorn, who had been murdered in 1463.

It therefore seems likely that the 1st Earl of Campbell – who acquired the castle through marriage around 1465 – gained a badly damaged tower, but one that was still relatively new. There are signs of damage and rebuilding, most noticeably in the first-floor hall, where the stonework in the east half looks to have suffered fire damage and the vault over the west half is clearly a rebuild.

Above: The castle seen in its setting above Dollar Glen.

Opposite: A drawing by R.W. Billings shows the castle from the east, around 1850. The roofs have not yet been restored, but the decorative water-spouts are still in place at the corners of the tower.

TIMELINE

c 1430	1463

CASTLE GLOOM built, possibly for John Stewart, Lord of Lorn.

WALTER STEWART sets fire to the castle, following the murder of John Stewart.

CLAN CAMPBELL

The Campbells had risen from comparative obscurity in the 13th century to become the most powerful clan in the western Highlands during the later Middle Ages. Their surname was originally spelt Cambel, derived from the Gaelic Caimbeul, 'wry or twisted mouth', a characteristic of one of their ancient chiefs. Later Campbell genealogies tell of the clan emerging from an earlier kindred called MacDuibne or Ó'Duibne ('sons of Duibne'), and even claim roots reaching back through the ancient Britons of Strathclyde to the legendary King Arthur.

Above: The Campbell coat of arms, depicting them as a seafaring clan.

The clan's rise to power effectively began when they allied themselves with Robert Bruce's cause during the Wars of Independence. Neil Campbell married Bruce's sister, Mary, after Bannockburn in 1314, whilst his son from an earlier relationship, Colin, was granted the lands of Loch Awe and Ardscotnish. Thereafter, the monarchy steadily built up the power of the Campbells in the problematic west. As royal lieutenants they were instrumental in the long and turbulent dismemberment of the empire of their sworn enemies, the MacDonald Lords of the Isles.

1465

COLIN CAMPBELL, 1ST EARL OF ARGYLL marries Isabel, daughter of John Stewart of Lorn, and acquires the castle and lands of Gloom.

1466

POPE PAUL II issues a bull condemning Walter Stewart's destruction of the 'Place of Glowm'.

The Campbells' earliest recorded stronghold in Argyll was Innis Chonnel, dramatically sited on an island in Loch Awe. Duncan, 1st Lord Campbell, oversaw the relocation to Inveraray, on Loch Fyne, prior to his death in 1453. By 1465, his son Colin had married Isabel, eldest daughter of John Stewart and heiress of Gloom. This allowed Colin to lay claim to Gloom – and brought the Campbells out of their Highland lair into the heart of the realm. But it was a disappointing outcome for Walter Stewart, whose bitterness was such that he attacked the castle. The papal rebuke that followed may well have been prompted by Earl Colin himself, who just happened to be on official business at the papal court in 1465–6.

DID YOU KNOW...

The Campbells are intimately associated with Argyllshire, but the first on record was Gillespic Campbell in 1263, who was granted lands in Menstrie and Sauchie, barely six miles (10km) from Castle Campbell.

Above: A view from the tower, looking south across the terraced gardens and Dollar Glen to the town of Dollar.

Left: Duncan Campbell, Lord of Loch Awe, who brought the Campbells to Inveraray, now the seat of the Campbells of Argyll.

FROM GLOOM TO CAMPBELL

E arl Colin's acquisition of Gloom was timely. He was a man on the up, largely thanks to his contribution to the downfall of the Black Douglases in 1455. A grateful James II belted him earl in 1457, and after the king's death in 1460, he became Master of the Household under James III. This post required him to be in almost constant attendance on the sovereign – thus he needed a secure but impressive residence at the heart of the kingdom. Gloom fitted the bill perfectly.

The tower would have served as Earl Colin's hall and private apartment, but there would also have been other buildings ranged around the courtyard, providing accommodation for his household and guests. These must have included a great hall for large-scale entertaining, and associated kitchen, and these may have occupied the old east range.

Below (left): The castle as it might have looked in the 16th century. The south range has been added, but the east range has not yet been remodelled.

Earl Colin was clearly pleased with his new residence. Following James IV's accession in 1488, Colin petitioned to have Gloom's name changed. The new king was indebted to the earl for helping him secure the throne and complied:

'OURE souverane Lord of his Riale autorite at the desire and Supplicacioun of his cousing and traist consalor Coline erle of Ergile, lord campbele and lorne his chancellare has chengeit the name of the castelle and place quhilk wes callit the Gloume pertenying to his said cousing … And ordinis the samyn castell to be callit in tyme to cum Campbele.'

NOBLE ADDITIONS

T he 1st Earl's descendants added to his residence, to suit changing fashions and circumstances. Archibald, the 2nd Earl, built the south range, with its splendid state apartment on the first floor, and probably added the terraced garden below. The south range bears a striking resemblance to the King's Old Building in Stirling Castle, built for James IV in the 1490s. This reminds us that Archibald moved in royal circles – he was chancellor from 1483 – and must have been influenced by his majesty's architectural tastes. He died alongside his king, and countless Campbells, at Flodden in 1513.

The new hall must have replaced the original great hall in the east range, which was then subdivided to create further accommodation. The next substantial enhancement at the castle was to this east range around 1590. Archibald, the 7th Earl, had the entire courtyard elevation rebuilt, adding the unusual two-bay loggia at ground level. By this date the old tower had long lost its role as lordly residence, and its first floor. The old hall was now serving as the 'lottar chalmer', or 'lettermeat hall' where the lower ranks of the household ate.

Above: The east range still retains part of its moulded string-course, marking the divisions between storeys.

1489

JAMES IV grants Earl Colin permission to change the castle's name from Gloom to Campbell.

c 1500

ARCHIBALD, 2ND EARL adds the south range, an impressive suite of rooms to befit his role as chancellor of Scotland.

CASTLE VISITORS

The castle would have hosted numerous important visitors during its heyday. They included two notable personalities in the time of Archibald, the 4th Earl (1529–58).

JOHN KNOX

Earl Archibald's religious sympathies were increasingly with the Protestant cause, and he was perhaps the first of the great noblemen to embrace the idea of Reformation with enthusiasm. And so it was that he invited John Knox to the castle, probably in 1556, four years before the Reformation Parliament of 1560.

Above: A drawing by R.W. Billings made around 1850 shows that the castle retained its ancient title long after the Campbells won the right to change it.

Left (below): John Knox, as depicted in a statue at the General Assembly Hall of the Church of Scotland in Edinburgh.

The fiery preacher had encountered problems soon after beginning his career in St Andrews in 1547, but following his return from exile in 1554 he gained strong support from Archibald Lord Lorn, Argyll's son and heir. According to Knox himself, he 'passed to the old Erle of Ergyle, who was then in the castell of campbell, where he taught certain dayis'.

According to tradition, Knox preached to a large congregation from the rocky knoll at the SW corner of the castle grounds, known as 'John Knox's Pulpit'. The small size of the knoll and the steep drops around it would have made it quite unsuited for large gatherings, and in all probability the scene of Knox's teaching was within the hall of the state apartment in the south range. Following his stay, Knox left Scotland for France and Geneva.

MARY QUEEN OF SCOTS

Seven years after Knox's visit, the castle welcomed an even more illustrious figure, Mary Queen of Scots. Mary stayed at the castle from 9 to 12 January 1563. She had come to attend the wedding of her kinsman James Stewart, Lord Doune, to Margaret, sister of the 5th Earl of Argyll. The festivities included banquets and masques; one of these involved guests dressing up as shepherds and playing lutes.

Two years later, however, Argyll had thrown in his lot with those who were in rebellion against the queen. In September 1565, Mary and Darnley, her second husband whom she had newly wed, passed close to Dollar Glen during their campaign against the rebels – the so-called 'Chaseabout Raid' – and received the surrender of the castle.

Above: Mary Queen of Scots, as depicted in a painting on display at Trinity House in Edinburgh.

1556	1563

REV JOHN KNOX preaches a Protestant sermon in the castle, four years before the Reformation.

MARY QUEEN OF SCOTS attends the wedding of the 5th Earl's sister at Castle Campbell.

THE CASTLE INVENTORY OF 1595

Castle Campbell would have been staffed at all times. When the lord was away, a skeleton staff would keep it secure and well maintained. But with the arrival of the lord, the whole complex would burst into life. His days here would be spent dealing with estate matters (he was responsible for law and order locally), or sporting in the surrounding hills. Many evenings would be occasions for feasting.

Standing in these draughty ruins, it is hard to visualise the castle's daily life. However, we are fortunate in having an inventory of the castle's 'inspreich and geir' (furnishings and property), drawn up in February 1595. It leads us through the castle, identifying each room by name and listing its contents.

Most usefully, it sheds light on the south range. Of the cellars identified, the one beside the garden pend was 'ye little sellar under ye kitchen', the next two were 'lairdnor' (larders) and the fourth the 'aill sellar' (ale cellar). The rooms on the first floor are named as 'hall', 'My Lordis uttir [outer] chalmer' and 'My Lordis Inner bed chalmer'. The more private rooms above were the 'common chalmer' and 'grein [green] chalmer'.

Above: A detail from one of the replica *Hunt of the Unicorn* tapestries at Stirling Castle. The tapestries listed on Castle Campbell's inventory may well have been of a similar style.

Opposite: The great hall as it might have looked in its heyday, with a banquet underway.

Opposite (below): The castle seen from the north.

1595

1638

AN INVENTORY is conducted at Castle Campbell. Among many items it records a mass cloth, plush furnishings and an iron yett similar to the one shown here.

THE NATIONAL COVENANT is signed in Edinburgh, in defiance of Charles I's imposition of Episcopalian worship.

At the west end of the hall were the 'kitchin' and 'pantrie' and above them two more floors housing single chambers.

Above the hall was 'ye wardrup' (wardrobe), a large storage space. Inside were beds, chairs and stools; tapestries, curtains and blankets; chandeliers, pots and pieces of armour. Other items include 'ye hie buird bordclayth' and 'ane buirdclat of arras work for ye buird in ye lottar chalmer' – tablecloths for the high table in the hall, and the table in the lettermeat hall. There was also 'ane fyne cramoise velvett mess clayth brouderit wit gold' (a fine crimson velvet Mass cloth embroidered with gold), which indicates there was a chapel here prior to the Protestant Reformation in 1560. In the 1640s, the Campbells were heavily involved in the Covenanters' struggle against the reimposition of Episcopalian worship.

Many items are listed under individual rooms. These include 'ane faldane comptar buird wit ane grit seatt at ye head of ye buird' (a folding counter table with a great seat at its head) in the lord's outer chamber, 'ane pair of kairt quheills' (cartwheels) in the 'girnell hous' (the cellar in the old hall) and, 'in ye passage to ye yaird', an iron yett.

A COVENANTING STRONGHOLD

Given the continuing support of the Campbell earls for the Protestant cause, it was inevitable that their castle would be drawn into the political and religious turmoil that dominated Scottish life in the 17th century. Archibald, 8th Earl, who was created Marquis by Charles I in 1641, subsequently played a conspicuous part in the Covenanters' cause against him.

Below: The castle in winter.

In 1645, the royalist leader, James Graham, Marquis of Montrose, made a triumphant progress from Fife to his last, and greatest, victory at Kilsyth. In the course of this campaign he took his army through Dollar. It is recorded that Montrose marched 'waistwards towards Striuelling and in his way he burnes the land of Castell Gloom otherways called Castell Campbell'.

Above: Archibald, 8th Earl and 1st Marquis of Argyll. Despite royal favour, he joined the Covenanters against Charles I.

The devastating attack on Dollar and Muckhart was apparently carried out by the MacLeans, who had long been at feud with the Campbells. The people of Dollar sought parliamentary recompense for the damage they endured, telling of 'whole houses … burnt, their corn destroyed, their bestiall and plenishing taken away … by enemies of this Kirke and kingdome in the rebellioun of James Graham and bloodie Irishes with him'.

It was long assumed that Castle Campbell had been destroyed by Montrose. However, while a party of MacLeans certainly hurled insults at the garrison, the castle remained in the Covenanters' hands, apparently little damaged. It was only a temporary reprieve, for the end of Castle Campbell was not far off.

1641

ARCHIBALD, 8TH EARL OF ARGYLL is created a marquis by Charles I. However, he soon joins the Covenanters' cause against the king.

1645

JAMES GRAHAM, 1ST MARQUIS OF MONTROSE lays waste to Dollar but, despite contemporary accounts of destruction, Castle Campbell is spared.

CROMWELL AND THE END

In September 1650, Oliver Cromwell's English army defeated the Scots at the Battle of Dunbar. His victory heralded another decade of turmoil for many Scots. Once again the Marquis of Argyll was at the centre of the action. Having placed the Scottish Crown on Charles II's head at Scone, on New Year's Day 1651, he promptly switched sides and was party to the proclamation of Cromwell as Lord Protector of Scotland.

Above: The coronation of Charles II at Scone, 1 January 1651. Archibald, 1st Marquis of Argyll, places the crown on the new king's head. He was later executed for his part in Charles I's demise.

Castle Campbell was inevitably caught up in the stirring events that followed. In 1653 Colonel Lilburne wrote to Cromwell from his base at Dalkeith: 'Hee [Argyll] promises to use his endeavour to his utmost power to preserve peace, and upon his return from Castle Cammel, which will be shortly, he will send for some of these new engagers, and try if he can convince them of their follie.' Shortly afterwards the castle was evidently garrisoned by English soldiers, since a requisition for bedding, blankets and such like, dated 26 December 1653, was issued to the burgesses of Culross.

The end of the castle came in 1654. General Monck, writing to Cromwell on 29 July from his base in Stirling, told how: 'wee are now come hither where wee shall stay some few days for refreshment. Some small parties of the Enemy are abroad in the country and on Monday and Tuesday nights last burnt Castle Campbell, an House belonging to the Marquise of Argyll.' Graphic evidence of this attack was found during excavations in the state apartment in 1982, when heavily charred floorboards and joists were found in the hall.

Above: General George Monck, Cromwell's commander-in-chief and later governor in Scotland. After Cromwell's death in 1658, he joined the royalist cause and helped restore Charles II to the throne.

1650

OLIVER CROMWELL invades Scotland. The Marquis of Argyll crowns Charles II at Scone the following year, but soon switches allegiance.

1654

CASTLE CAMPBELL razed by royalists, furious that Argyll allowed Cromwell's forces to use it as a base.

A NEW LOWLAND SEAT

T he Marquis of Argyll may have planned to repair the damage when more peaceful times returned. He never got the chance. In 1661, the year after Charles II returned to his thrones, Argyll was executed for treason. His son, to whom the earldom but not the marquisate was restored in 1663, chose to forsake Castle Campbell for a more amenable, and more easily accessible, residence in Stirling. He acquired a magnificent town house beside Stirling Castle formerly belonging to the 1st Earl of Stirling, and remodelled it to form the house now known as Argyll's Lodging.

Below (left:) Argyll's Lodging, near Stirling Castle, which replaced Castle Campbell as chief residence of the 9th Earl of Argyll.

Castle Campbell was left to fall into ruin. It was briefly garrisoned with a small force by the 2nd Duke of Argyll during the 1715 Jacobite Rising, but in 1805 the 6th Duke sold it to Mr Crawford Tait, owner of the neighbouring Harvieston estate. Clan Campbell's long connection with the castle that still bears their name had ended.

1661

THE MARQUIS OF ARGYLL executed for treason. It is said he sleeps peacefully on the final night of his life.

1663

ARCHIBALD, 9TH EARL OF ARGYLL abandons Castle Campbell for the Stirling town house known as Argyll's Lodging.

THE CASTLE IN THE GLEN

During the 18th and 19th centuries the impressive ruin above Dollar Glen came to be increasingly appreciated for its picturesque beauty, and many romantic images were made of it. In 1874–5 Sir James Orr of Harvieston carried out archaeological investigations among the ruins and took measures to prevent further decay. In 1948 Mr Kerr of Harvieston entrusted the castle and glen into the care of the National Trust for Scotland, and an agreement was reached whereby the Trust would maintain the glen whilst the Ministry of Works (Historic Scotland's predecessor) would care for the castle. Since then the ruins have been stabilised, and a new roof placed on the ancient tower.

Above: The castle from the north in 1945.

Below: The Glasgow businessman Sir Andrew Orr, who bought Castle Campbell in 1859.

Castle Campbell is one of dozens of Historic Scotland sites in central Scotland, a selection of which is shown below.

Stirling Castle

↗ In Stirling off the M9

🕐 Open all year

📞 01786 450 000

🚗 Approx. 10 miles from Castle Campbell

Linlithgow Palace

↗ In Linlithgow off the M9

🕐 Open all year

📞 01506 842 896

🚗 Approx. 12 miles from Castle Campbell

Doune Castle

↗ In Doune, 10 miles NW of Stirling on the A84

🕐 Open all year (Winter: closed Thu & Fri)

📞 01786 841 742

🚗 Approx. 15 miles from Castle Campbell

Lochleven Castle

↗ Reached by boat from Kinross off the M90

🕐 Open summer only

📞 07778 040 483

🚗 Approx. 10 miles from Castle Campbell

For more information on all Historic Scotland sites, visit **www.historic-scotland.gov.uk**
To order tickets and a wide range of gifts, visit **www.historic-scotland.gov.uk/shop**

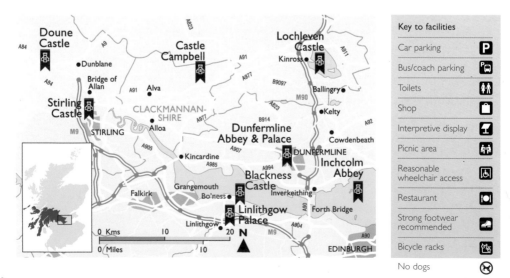

Key to facilities

Car parking	P
Bus/coach parking	P🚌
Toilets	👫
Shop	🛍
Interpretive display	🖼
Picnic area	🧺
Reasonable wheelchair access	♿
Restaurant	🍽
Strong footwear recommended	👢
Bicycle racks	🚲
No dogs	🚫